EXPLORERS OF
THE AMERICAS
BEFORE COLUMBUS

Explorers of the Americas Before Columbus

George deLucenay Leon

FRANKLIN WATTS / 1989
NEW YORK / LONDON / TORONTO / SYDNEY

Maps by Joe Le Monnier

Photographs courtesy of:
U.S. Geological Survey: p. 12; The Bettmann Archive, Inc.:
pp. 16 (top and bottom), 44 (top and bottom), 50, 56;
United Nations: p. 20; Denver Museum of Natural History:
p. 23; Board Failte Photo: pp. 26, 28; The Granger Collection:
pp. 33, 39; New York Public Library Picture Collection: p. 47.

Library of Congress Cataloging-in-Publication Data
Leon, George deLucenay.
Explorers of the Americas before Columbus / George deLucenay Leon.
p.   cm.—(A First book)
Bibliography: p.
Includes index.
Summary: Examines the voyages of explorers who reached the shores of
North America before Columbus. Discusses Eric the Red, Leif Ericsson,
the Norse settlements, and ancient visitors to South and Latin America.
ISBN 0-531-10667-5
1. America—Discovery and exploration—Pre-Columbian—Juvenile literature.
2. Explorers—America—History—Juvenile literature. [1. America—Discovery
and exploration—Pre-Columbian. 2. Explorers.] I. Title. II. Series.
E103.L47   1989
970.1'1—dc19   88-30336   CIP   AC

CONTENTS

EXPLORERS OF THE AMERICAS BEFORE COLUMBUS

1

EXPLORERS OF THE NEW WORLD BEFORE COLUMBUS

We usually think of Christopher Columbus as the discoverer of the New World. But although his four historic voyages made him a household name, other explorers reached these shores many years before Columbus first crossed the Atlantic Ocean in 1492. Some settled here. Others stayed a short while, then left.

Besides the explorers whom we know for certain came here, other explorers may have arrived as well. Some of the voyages are described in legends handed down through the centuries, both in the Old World and the New World. Scientists and nonscientists alike also suggest that ancient voyages explain certain mysteries or coincidences—for example, uncanny similarities among distant cultures.

On trips of long ago—whether real or mythical—daring explorers navigated through uncharted territories on land and sea. They were unaware of the dangers in their path and ignorant of what they might find. On the sea, invisible reefs could tear out the bottom of a ship. A storm could spring up without warning. Giant sea monsters could pull a ship to the bottom of the ocean. On land, wild animals could attack a hunting party. Unknown people could kill a ship's crew or wipe out an expeditionary party. A ship might fall off the edge of the earth, which, at that time, was believed to be flat.

Today's explorers, whether of mountains, oceans, or space, have the benefit of technological and human support. Climbers scaling Mt. Everest usually have support teams and high-tech equipment. Astronauts rely on hundreds of scientists, engineers, and technicians on earth and on sophisticated computers and other equipment.

But the early explorers of the Americas had only their brains, simple tools, and the other members of their group, family, crew, or tribe to aid them. This was all they had to brave the elements and the unknown. Nevertheless, they managed to get there, settle, and establish civilizations all their own.

2

THE FIRST
AMERICANS

About 3.5 to 4 million years ago, the climate on earth started to change slowly. The winters gradually grew longer and colder. More snow fell. The snow on the ground took longer to melt in spring and summer.

Eventually, snow began to stay on the ground all year round in many places. Over the years it began piling up. The snow was so packed that it became ice. Year-round snowfields and ice masses increased in size. In places the ice formed glaciers—huge sheets as much as 2 miles (3 km) thick and thousands of miles long and wide.

Eventually, the snowfall began to decrease, and the process reversed. The temperature of the earth warmed up a little. Less precipitation fell, and the glaciers began to melt and decrease in size.

Then the earth cooled again, causing the glaciers to grow once more. At least three such warming periods—and at least four glacial periods—occurred during the past million years.

Millions of years ago, the earth was covered with glaciers, like this one in Alaska.

The period characterized by extensive movement of ice sheets is called the Pleistocene Epoch, or Ice Age. During the glacial periods, ice covered Siberia, northern Europe, and parts of North America as far south as the Mississippi Valley. Perhaps a third of the earth was covered with ice. New England was under an ice sheet 1 mile (1.6 km) high. Today, you can see signs of this early glacial activity throughout the upper half of the United States.

Glaciers still exist in North America. There are some big glaciers in Alaska and northern Canada, and smaller ones on mountaintops in the Rockies and Cascades. These glaciers increase and decrease in size depending on the amount of snowfall each year, but they show no signs of turning into the massive glaciers of thousands of years ago.

Some scientists believe that the Ice Age has not ended and that we are now in an interglacial period.

Of Ice and Humans

During this period, both human beings and animals began moving east. The larger animals, such as mammoths and bison, were probably searching for new grazing grounds; close on their heels were their predators—cave bears, tigers, and humans.

Tribes from Asia eventually migrated to the Chukchi Peninsula, the point of land in Siberia closest to the North American continent. Probably several times over a period of perhaps as long as thirty thousand years, when travel was easiest, they crossed what is now called the Bering Strait to the North American continent.

The animals also crossed the Strait. Mammoths— huge ancestors of elephants—were the favorite target of human hunters. A male mammoth weighed 6 or more tons

(5,500 kg) and measured 10 to 14 feet (3 to 4 m) at the shoulder. A single mammoth could provide plenty of meat for many families, as well as ivory for tools and weapons. Humans also wore the hides and fur of other animals, and they turned their ivory and bones into needles, spearheads, and other tools and weapons.

How did humans and animals cross 125 miles (200 km) of water? Quite simply. At the time of the crossing, a land bridge, now called Beringia, existed across the present Bering Strait. The land bridge between Asia and North America was huge, over 1,200 miles (2,000 km) at its widest point; during periods of glaciation, the ocean level was about 450 feet (140 m) lower than it is today. During warming periods, glacial melting raised the level of the oceans and the present Strait covered the land bridge.

With all the game available, the hunters rarely went hungry. Families grew larger. They spread out, covering more and more territory.

Some of the immigrants settled in what is now called the Yukon Territory (in Canada) and Alaska. Others continued south. As each wave of immigrants arrived, they crowded those who had arrived earlier. Then the first wave would move farther south, or the new wave would keep going past the earlier group.

Eventually some people moved all the way east to the eastern coast of North America, from Newfoundland to Florida. Others continued south until they reached Tierra del Fuego, the southernmost tip of South America. Human bones and other evidence of human habitation have been found in Tierra del Fuego that date to as far back as ten thousand years ago.

Scientists believe that people in early societies moved no farther than they had to. This was usually about 17 miles (27 km) per generation. Traveling the 7,000 miles

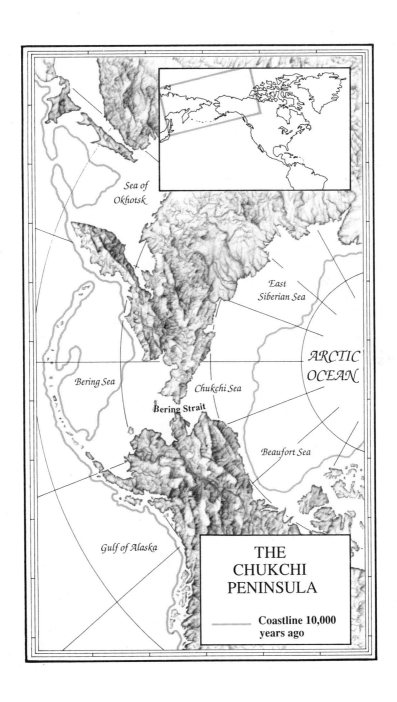

Sea of
Okhotsk

East
Siberian Sea

ARCTIC
OCEAN

Bering Sea

Chukchi Sea

Bering Strait

Beaufort Sea

Gulf of Alaska

THE
CHUKCHI
PENINSULA

Coastline 10,000
years ago

The ancestors of this Eskimo mother and child were among the earliest immigrants to the New World.

Some scientists believe that the American Indian descended from the early Asians who crossed the Bering Strait.

(11,000 km) from Chukchi to the tip of South America at that rate would have taken about four hundred generations, or over eight thousand years.

What happened to the early Americans? Most scientists believe that the people we call Indians or Native Americans are descended from these ancient Asians. The Mayans, Aztecs, and Incas, as well as their descendants, also share these ancestors.

3

SCIENTISTS MEET THE FIRST AMERICANS

How can we know that something happened thousands of years ago if no one was there to write it down?

Digging Up the Past

We learn about ancient peoples, about where and how they lived, by studying the remains of their cultures. These remains, called artifacts, include their bones, the bones of animals they killed, their campsites, their graves, their cave paintings, and their tools and weapons. To the archaeologist—the scientist who looks for clues to the existence of early peoples—these artifacts tell a story. Sometimes this story is almost as clear as if someone had written it down.

Most artifacts are found only by digging for them. The artifacts of very old cultures may be many feet under the ground. However, archaeologists may discover a few artifacts above ground that tip them off to discoveries of many more artifacts underground. Erosion can wear away

To learn about the past, archaeologists
explore the sites of ancient civilizations.
Here, excavations are taking place at
a Mayan ruin in Guatemala.

the soil and rock that cover old campsites, for example, exposing a piece of stone flaked by human hands or a group of rocks in the shape of a hearth.

An open site—12,000 years old—was discovered near Folsom, New Mexico in the late 1920s. The earth had not been disturbed for centuries. This site was ideal because the ancient artifacts—arrowheads and bones of animals—had not been mixed with newer ones.

The archaeologists dug carefully in the cave, sifting every spadeful of earth through fine sieves. A tiny bit of bone could prove important. The archaeologists discovered a bison's head in which projectiles had lodged.

Several ancient hearths were also unearthed, and in them antelope bones were found. The people who killed the antelopes most likely cooked the meat. These Ancient people were probably hunters and not farmers.

Dating the Past

A bone found 20 feet (6 m) underground is usually older than one found 10 feet (3.5 m) underground. But how do scientists know the actual age of each bone? They use a method called either radiocarbon dating or the carbon 14 method.

Every organism absorbs carbon in the process of living. The air you breathe contains carbon dioxide, for example, and all the food you eat contains carbon. Some of this carbon—a very small amount—is radioactive. Radioactive carbon is deposited in your bones, in the bones of animals, and in the parts of plants.

An organism that dies stops absorbing radioactive carbon. Then, instead of becoming progressively more radioactive, it becomes progressively less radioactive.

Scientists burn a bit of an object that used to be alive or part of a living organism to determine its age. The burning produces carbon dioxide gas, and a radiation counter is used to measure the amount of radioactivity in the gas. The radioactivity is produced by the radiocarbon in the sample. The less radiation, the older the sample.

This method will not tell you that a tree was cut down exactly 3,466 years ago. But it will tell you that the tree was cut down about 3,400 years ago, plus or minus 100 years or so. That means the tree was cut down between 3,300 and 3,500 years ago.

Other techniques are also used to date artifacts. One involves the analysis of amino acids—the building blocks of proteins—in the remains of living matter. Another involves the study of pollen grains.

Studying the Earliest Americans

As you know, scientists have evidence of the ancient habitation of North America. The existence of prehistoric humans in North America has been documented by the analysis of bones, tools, campsites, and other artifacts. Twelve-thousand-year-old arrowhead points have been found in New Mexico. A piece of a basket believed to be almost twenty thousand years old has been found near Pittsburgh. Human bones dated at twenty-three thousand years have been found near Los Angeles.

But why do we believe that the earliest Americans came here from Asia? The similarity between old arrowheads or spear points found in both North and South America and those found in Asia is the clue. In particular, points found near Folsom and Clovis, New Mexico, have characteristics unmistakably resembling points found in parts of Asia. The points found in the New World are also quite sophisticated. This indicates that their makers brought with them a fairly advanced culture.

*An artifact discovered in
Folsom, New Mexico. Un-
earthed relics tell us a great
deal about ancient cultures.*

Scientists know that the shape of a spear point is like a trademark. Each group of people made their spear points in only one way, and at different periods in ancient history people formed their spear points in distinctive ways. Studying spearheads (and other tools and artifacts) enables scientists to tell at what period and where the makers of the spear points lived.

4

ST. BRENDAN
AND THE
NEW FOUND
LAND

According to Irish legend and old manuscripts, an Irish priest named Brendan took a boat ride in the sixth century A.D. from his homeland to what is now called Newfoundland, a province of Canada.

Brendan lived at a time when the Catholic Church actively encouraged missionaries to bring Christianity to parts of the world inhabited by non-Christians. This was also a time when many Christians became hermits and went to live in uninhabited or sparsely inhabited places. Other missionaries visited these far-flung missions and hermitages to bring news and supplies, keep track of progress at the missions, and in general lend their support to the outposts.

Brendan was one of those who checked up on the Church's missionaries and hermits. He was known to have visited Iceland, Brittany (in northern France), and Spain. He was so dedicated to his work that after his death he was canonized. He became known as St. Brendan.

His Newfoundland voyage—if it did take place—would have been difficult, to say the least. Little if anything was known in Europe about a land to the far west. Stories told of a place called the Heavenly Isles to the west of Ireland, but we do not know if this referred to any real place.

Equally daunting was the type of boat Brendan would have had to travel in. He would have used a curragh, or coracle. This tiny boat, still used in Ireland today, has a framework of wooden strips covered with greased cowhides stitched together. Its construction is similar to that of an old-fashioned canvas canoe and is not well suited for long and rough ocean voyages.

A tiny boat like this, called a curragh, was used by the Irish explorer Brendan to travel to Newfoundland.

The North Atlantic is notorious for its sudden storms, icy gales, and icebergs. Nevertheless, old manuscripts say that Brendan, along with seventeen other priests, made a journey to the New World about fourteen hundred years ago. The trip—whether real or made up—was well documented.

The priests saw a "column of crystal"—probably an iceberg. They were approached by a huge monster spouting water—probably a curious whale. At one point in their voyage they managed to break the monotony of their diet of cold food by building a fire on a large flat black rock that they found in the middle of the ocean. Unfortunately the rock was the back of a whale. The whale dived, taking along with it the fire and dinner.

As Brendan and his fellow travelers passed one body of land, they encountered a hail of stones and saw steam rising from both the earth and the water. They could have been passing Iceland, which has active volcanoes and a lot of steam vents. They continued traveling until they landed on a distant western shore.

According to various versions of the legend, the whole trip took anywhere from two to five years. (Presumably they were not at sea the whole time, since the actual distance is not that far!) A trip from Ireland to Newfoundland might have followed ocean currents. An ocean current is like a river in the ocean. A ship in such a current is carried along with or without the assistance of sails or paddles.

The legends do not say where Brendan landed, but they do say he was welcomed by people who knew him by name. This would mean that a missionary outpost was already located on the North American continent. Presumably the people these missionaries were trying to convert were Indians—perhaps the descendants of the migrants who long before had fled the numbing cold of the Ice Age.

Timothy Severin, an Irish sailor, sailed this ship in 1976 to recreate Brendan's trip to Newfoundland.

If the voyage of Brendan did indeed occur, we might expect to find artifacts along the way in the places he stopped—tools, buildings, graves. But such artifacts have never been found. However, we do know that missions were established. And in spite of seemingly impossible conditions, experienced mariners just might have been able to overcome the limitations of the small boats, harsh conditions, and lack of maps. Of course, if missions had already been established as far away as Newfoundland, maps might have existed but just not survived.

In 1976, fourteen hundred years after the voyage of Brendan, Timothy Severin, an Irish sailor, left Ireland on a boat trip to prove that Brendan's trip was possible. Severin's boat was a coracle, made exactly like Brendan's. It was 36 feet (11 m) long and had masts 12 and 19 feet (3.7 and 5.8 m) high and two sails. Forty-nine tanned ox-hides soaked in grease were stitched together with leather thongs and attached to a wicker frame. Each hide measured 45 by 47 inches (114 by 119 cm). Oars 12 feet (3.7 m) long provided steering and locomotion. Severin called his boat *Brendan*.

Severin made the first leg of his trip to Iceland with three companions. On May 7, 1977, after learning more about handling the coracle, he and his friends left Reykjavik, Iceland, bound for Newfoundland. After going through storms and ice floes and having to sew up a punctured hull in freezing water, they eventually reached their destination about six weeks later, on June 26.

Whether or not Brendan himself did reach the New World, we now know that such a trip was indeed in the realm of possibility.

5

THE VIKINGS

In A.D. 982, a Viking chieftain named Eric Thorvaldsson (pronounced *Eric Torvald-son*)—better known as Eric the Red, because of his red hair—killed two men in a quarrel and was exiled from his home in Iceland. During his exile he heard stories about an island lying somewhere to the west of Iceland. He decided to look for this island. He found it and spent three years exploring it.

Eventually, he was allowed to return to Iceland, and when he did, he told the people of his discovery. The island, he said, was suitable for raising sheep and other livestock. The land was fertile, the sea filled with fish, and the summers warm. He called the island Greenland.

The Vikings

The Vikings—also called Norsemen—lived in the part of the world now known as Scandinavia, which includes the countries of Sweden, Norway, and Denmark. They also lived on the island we now call Iceland.

Until the end of the eighth century A.D., most Norsemen were peaceful farmers, ranchers, fishermen, or traders. They were famous for their shipbuilding and sailing abilities.

Toward the end of the eighth century, many Vikings began to leave their homeland in search of more and better land. Many also were drawn by dreams of riches and glory. Viking pirates began raiding towns and monasteries in foreign lands.

A Norse chieftain would gather members of his clan and fill his ship with warriors. In their dragon ships—as they were called because they had high prows carved in the shape of a serpent—the Vikings sailed up and down the coasts of Spain, Italy, and France raiding villages. They even went as far east as Constantinople.

Sometimes the Vikings found a place that was lightly populated and settled there. They did this in northern France, which to this day is called Normandy, after the Norsemen. A Norse tribe called the Rus settled in what is now Kiev in the Soviet Union. The name Russia comes from their name.

Other Vikings were blown off course in their ships and wound up in previously unknown lands—something that was considered lucky. Vikings blown off course during a storm came upon Iceland between A.D. 850 and 870. Although the lucky Vikings found conditions on Iceland little better than those on the mainland, within sixty years sixty thousand people were living there.

Eric the Red

Eric the Red, the discoverer of Greenland, came from a line of skilled mariners experienced in sailing through the gales common in the northern seas. Huge waves could sweep over the ships in these waters. Icy winds whipped freezing spray into the mariners' faces. A ship might ride to the top of a wave and then plunge down the other side. Over the years the Vikings had made their ships capable of withstanding such battering. They had also perfected their sailing skills. As someone once said, "The crew is more important than the boat."

Eric chose the name for his island carefully. He wanted to encourage people to move there.

The discovery
of Greenland by
the Vikings

Move they did. Under his leadership, at least twenty-five boats containing about four hundred people left Iceland in 985 or 986 to make the voyage to Greenland. In the course of their voyage they ran into bad weather; only fourteen of the ships arrived safely. Some of the boats had to turn back; others were wrecked and sank.

Greenland was not what the settlers had expected. For eight months of the year they had to stay indoors because of the intense cold. Crops would not ripen, and the island was often surrounded by pack ice, which prevented them from taking the boats out for fishing.

Greenland—the largest island in the world—has about the same climate as Maine does today. But a thousand years ago, the weather was noticeably colder than it is now (although nowhere near as cold as it was during an Ice Age). The summers were too short for a good wheat crop, and there were few green meadows on which to graze cattle and sheep. All in all, the new settlers had been fooled by Eric. He was like a real estate agent who describes the beauty of a house without mentioning the leaky roof.

Bjarni Sees the New World—
And Turns Back

The same year that Eric the Red returned to Greenland—985 or 986—another Icelander, Bjarni Herjolfsson (*Bee-year-nee Hair-yolf-son*), went to Norway for the summer. When he returned to Iceland, he found that his father had sold the family farm and gone as part of the expedition just described.

To rejoin his father, Bjarni gathered a crew that autumn and set sail for Greenland. Autumn is the worst time of the year to be on the waters of the northern Atlantic. The crew was probably constantly wet. They may have been unable to cook their food. Fog may have made it impossible to navigate. They may have had near misses with icebergs looming out of the fog.

The Vikings steered by the sun and stars, having no compasses. On cloudy or foggy days they could not get their bearings. Bjarni and his crew didn't see the sun for four days. When the sun did come up, they continued sailing west. However, they really weren't sure where they were.

Eventually, they sighted land. At first they were overjoyed. But as they came closer, Bjarni realized that it was not Greenland. There were no glaciers. Instead of mountains, there were tiny hills. He sailed on for two more days. Another coast appeared. It too bore no resemblance to the coast of Greenland that had been described.

The crew wanted to stop and visit the land anyway, but Bjarni insisted on turning back at once. He probably had sighted the eastern coast of Canada, but he missed the opportunity of being the first Viking to land on it.

The Sagas

The voyages of Eric and Bjarni are recounted in sagas, or stories. These sagas tell the history of Icelandic and Norwegian kings and chieftains and their families. They were told through the centuries to pass the time during the long Scandinavian nights. Eventually, they were written down in the language we call Old Norse.

Two sagas that tell of Eric and Bjarni are *The Greenlanders' Saga* and *Erik the Red's Saga*. These were written down in the fourteenth and fifteenth centuries, but were based on material from older manuscripts. Other written sources also exist, some even older than these two sagas.

Although sagas are stories and contain fictional material, many of their elements have been documented as true by historians and scientists.

GREENLAND

Cumberland Peninsula

Hall Peninsula

Greenland Sea

Labrador Sea

LABRADOR

NEWFOUNDLAND

Cape Breton Island

Nova Scotia

ATLANTIC OCEAN

Barent's Sea

Norwegian Sea

ICELAND

North Sea

IRELAND

THE NORTH ATLANTIC OF
THE EARLY EXPLORERS

The Voyage of Leif Ericsson

Late in the tenth century, another Viking bought Bjarni's boat and set sail for the land Bjarni had seen. He believed, as did many others, that a boat *knew* where it had been and could find its way back there. Among his crew of thirty-five were some of the crew from the original voyage. The Viking leader was Leif Ericsson, the son of Eric the Red (Ericsson means "son of Eric").

After many days at sea, Leif and his crew arrived at an island they called Helluland, which means "Stone" or "Crag Land." This island, on which they sighted glaciers, was probably Baffin Island. They continued to sail south and reached a land covered with trees and white, sandy beaches. Leif named this place Markland—"Forest Land." This may have been the coast of Labrador or just another peninsula of Baffin Island.

They eventually reached a place with grass and trees. The crew built huts and wintered there. They found the winter mild compared with that of Greenland. Leif called this land Vinland, which is usually translated "Land of Grapevines" but possibly means "Pastureland." Vinland was probably northern Newfoundland.

According to the sagas, the travelers then decided to return home. The frozen ocean was now free of pack ice. Leif ordered timber to be cut and loaded onto the boat, as well as cattle fodder. This may have been to prove to people that he had indeed found land that had trees and that was suitable for grazing.

A short time after Leif returned to Greenland, his brother Thorvald led another expedition to the New World. Thorvald was killed by Indians, and his crew returned to Greenland the following spring.

Later the Icelander Thorfinn Karlsefni led a trip to the New World that included three ships, between 60 and 160

*The landing of Leif Ericsson on
the shores of Vinland in 985*

men and women, and livestock. He stayed there three
winters and then left, probably because of hostilities between the Vikings and the Indians. Other voyages were
made to the New World over the next three hundred or
so years, but no longstanding colonies were ever established, as they had been in Greenland.

There are speculations that during their presence in
the New World, the Vikings explored different parts of
Canada as well as the coast of America as far south as
Florida. But no solid evidence exists for most of these
speculations.

The Norse Settlements

Until 1964, no proof existed that Vikings had landed in the New World and set up a colony. However, many historians and archaeologists nonetheless believed that Vikings had reached the New World.

In 1964, Helge Ingstad, a Norwegian historian, and his archaeologist wife, Anne Stine Ingstad, reported finding a Norse site at the northernmost tip of Newfoundland in a place now called L'Anse aux Meadows. This site was found to contain the ruins of a small Viking village. There were eight long houses and four or five boathouses, along with several cooking pits, a smithy, a charcoal kiln, and deposits of bog iron. The Ingstads found the remains of post holes where logs had been driven into the ground. These logs had supported the walls of a house in exactly the same way the Norse are known to have built their houses.

An analysis of artifacts using the radiocarbon method dated the settlement at about A.D. 1000. Although it is certain that the Vikings did have a settlement at L'Anse aux Meadows, it is not known whether this was the camp of Leif Ericsson or his brother Thorvald or the settlement of Karlsefni.

The Legacy of the Vikings

The Vikings' great age of exploration lasted for about two hundred years. New World explorations continued for another 350 years. Viking settlements on Greenland were maintained until the end of the fifteenth century. At their height, about three thousand people inhabited these settlements.

What is the legacy of these pioneering Vikings? We do have Leif's sailing directions to the New World, but

Baffin Bay

BAFFIN ISLAND

GREENLAND

Hudson Strait

L'Anse aux Meadows

Kap Farvel

Hudson Bay

LABRADOR

Cape Harrison

NEWFOUNDLAND

Cape Breton

NOVA SCOTIA

Cape Cod

NORTH
AMERICA

Cape May

because he did not know of the compass, we can't use his information to determine where he went. Norse directions went something like this: "Three days sail on a southwesterly course. Then when a point of land is seen we turn so we see it on our right for two more days. When we see such and such a peak we head toward the setting sun." Modern scholars have been unable to use such directions to reconstruct the voyages of Leif and others.

If the Vikings didn't make their own maps, others did, based on information provided by the Vikings. These maps were known in the sailing centers in Italy, Portugal, Spain, and England. Because they assumed the world was flat, not round, people thought—incorrectly—that India and China could be reached by sailing westward from Europe.

As a master mariner, Columbus would have studied all the information he could find on westward trips. That is why he sailed westward to find lands that in reality lay to the east of Europe.

6

ANCIENT
VISITORS TO
LATIN AMERICA

About fourteen hundred years before the birth of Christ, a civilization began to develop along the Gulf of Mexico that became remarkably complex in a short span. Because Olmec civilization seemed to appear suddenly (it could not have developed from neighboring advanced cultures because there were none), some scientists believe it was influenced by people from other parts of the world. Scientists and historians who support theories that the Olmecs and other American cultures were so influenced are called diffusionists. They believe that some elements of certain cultures diffused there rather than develop by themselves.

One of the most distinctive products of Olmec culture are the giant rock heads they carved and carted 80 miles (130 km) to their present sites. These heads are 6 to 9 feet (2 to 3 m) tall and weigh up to 40 tons (36 mt).

Some people believe the Olmecs were influenced by the ancient Phoenicians, whose culture was developed at about the same time. The Phoenicians were the greatest

This tremendous rock head is one of the more unique products of the Olmec culture, which existed 1400 B.C.

The Phoenicians sailed in great ships like these, but there is no proof that they actually landed in the New World.

mariners of their time and were the first to travel all the way around Africa—a three-year voyage. They traded with England, exchanging their lumber, cloth, bronze, and furniture for tin.

Supporters of this theory argue that, guided by the wind and following ocean currents, ships theoretically could have made the voyage from the Mediterranean to the Gulf of Mexico. Among the ships' crews may have been Africans—probably slaves—with features similar to those of some of the Olmec heads. The features seem to be those of black Africans rather than American Indians.

No proof exists that the Phoenicians actually reached the New World, but as you will read in the next chapter, such a voyage was indeed within the realm of possibility.

Other evidence points to Chinese influence. For example, the Chinese of this period were experts in working with jade, a green semiprecious stone. The Olmecs, too, were expert workers of jadelike stones.

The Feathered Serpent

Two other important cultures arose "south of the border." In the steamy jungles of southern Mexico and northern Central America, Mayan culture began to develop as early as 1500 B.C. and reached its peak about A.D. 880. More recently, in the valley of Mexico to the north, the Aztecs flourished. Their culture peaked in the late fifteenth century and early sixteenth century. Both cultures had sophisticated calendars, writing systems, pyramids, and economies. Both cultures also had many gods, one of whom was similar.

Kulkulcan, one of the most important Mayan gods, was said to have brought people the gifts of corn and farming. Statues represent him as a feathered serpent.

The Aztecs also worshipped a god depicted as a feathered serpent—Quetzalcoatl (*Qwet-zal-co-at-ell*). Although Quetzalcoatl means "feathered serpent," some codices (manuscript books) depict Quetzalcoatl as a bearded man.

Both the Mayans and the Aztecs shared a legend that Kulkulcan/Quetzalcoatl was a man who crossed the Atlantic Ocean centuries before and came to their shores. The Aztecs believed that Quetzalcoatl stopped the sacrifices of humans and taught the tribes to live in peace. He also brought the seeds of maize—corn. Quetzalcoatl then left but promised to return one day.

When Hernando Cortés arrived in the land of the Aztecs in the sixteenth century, he found out about the legend and said he was Quetzalcoatl returning as promised. His ruse helped him conquer the mighty Aztecs with only a handful of soldiers.

Ivan van Sertima, a linguist (person who studies languages) with an interest in different cultures, believes that the "real" Quetzalcoatl was originally based not on a mythical god but on a real person who was one of a shipload of sailors who visited these shores in the fourteenth century A.D. The sailors were from a mighty West African kingdom called Mali.

Arab traders told the leader of Mali, Abukhari II, about a great body of water to the west and about a land on the other side of this ocean. Fired by the story, Abukhari outfitted ships for the journey and commanded his captains to locate this land and report back to him. He waited and waited, but the ships never returned.

Not to be discouraged, he outfitted another fleet. This time he commanded the fleet himself. This was early in the fourteenth century. Abukhari would have picked up the Canary current and followed it to southern Mexico or Guatemala.

*Quetzalcoatl—
the Aztec god*

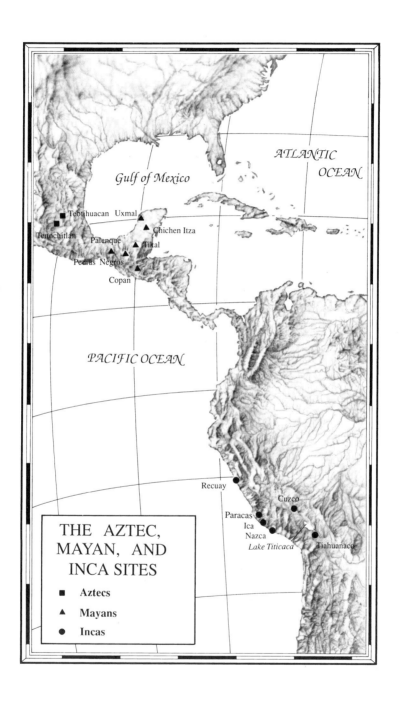

THE AZTEC,
MAYAN, AND
INCA SITES

■ **Aztecs**

▲ **Mayans**

● **Incas**

Transoceanic voyages such as this may also explain apparent similarities between words and symbols of American cultures and cultures of other continents. They may also explain the presence in the New World of crops such as cotton. Cotton did not originate in the New World, but it has been cultivated there for a long time. Did Egyptian travelers bring it to the New World?

Ancient Visitors
to South America

The ancient people of Peru also had legends of visitors to South America.

One of their stories goes like this:

In the land that is now Peru, long before the Spanish conquerors devastated the country, the people were warlike, lived in caves, and dressed in leaves or covered themselves with animal hides. They knew nothing about farming.

One day there appeared a tall white, bearded man dressed in long flowing garments. A girdle was tied about his middle, and his hair was cut in the same way that Spanish friars cut theirs. His followers dressed in a similar fashion. He taught the Indians to live in peace and to terrace the mountainous country so they could plant vegetables. He gave them the gifts of corn and cotton. He also showed them how to weave wool and cotton to make clothes.

These foreigners built their dwellings on the island of Titicaca, which is still considered a sacred place by Indians today. The white leader also had a stepped pyramid called a ziggurat built close to the lake shore at Tiahuanaco (*Tia-wan-aco*). One day he departed but promised to return.

*A depiction of an Inca cere-
mony worshipping the sun*

The Indians worshipped him, and in some parts of that vast country he and his followers were named Viracocha (*Veer-a-coach-a*), or "sea foam people." In other places he was called Kon, and in still others, Tiki. Both names mean "ruler" or "chief."

Much later, Quechua (*Kay-chew-a*) Indians dominated the land under their leader, called the Inca. They kept the white leader and his teachings fresh in their minds by combining the three names and calling him Kon-Tiki Viracocha.

Spaniards arriving in Peru in the middle of the sixteenth century were treated graciously by the Inca, who thought these white, bearded strangers were the god and his followers returning from across the water. Too late, the Inca and his people found that all the strangers wanted was to seize their gold. The outcome was the same as in Mexico. The Spaniards killed and enslaved the people and took their gold and precious jewels. They also destroyed their historical records.

Archaeologists working in the jungles of Central and South America are constantly learning new things about the great civilizations of the past. Will we ever fully understand the origins of these civilizations and the myths and legends they developed? Someday we may. Until then, we have to content ourselves with some facts, some stories, some far-flung theories, and the work of our imaginations.

7

THE RA
EXPEDITIONS

In 1968, Thor Heyerdahl, a descendant of the Vikings, set out to demonstrate that ships built before the time of Columbus could have made the voyage from the Old World to the New. Heyerdahl had been fascinated by resemblances between cultures separated not just by distance but by oceans as well.

He built his ship from reeds and modeled it after ships depicted on ancient Egyptian wall paintings. These murals, painted about five thousand years ago, show the entire construction process of Egyptian ships. Heyerdahl was able to use these paintings as blueprints.

His ship was built from reeds that grew in the Egyptian marshes. Reeds were secured with more reeds into long, flexible bunches the thickness of a person's wrist, and these bunches were in turn lashed together into larger bunches. No nails were used, and a single sail was mounted, just as shown in the murals. A ship built in such a way might seem unable to withstand the constant bat-

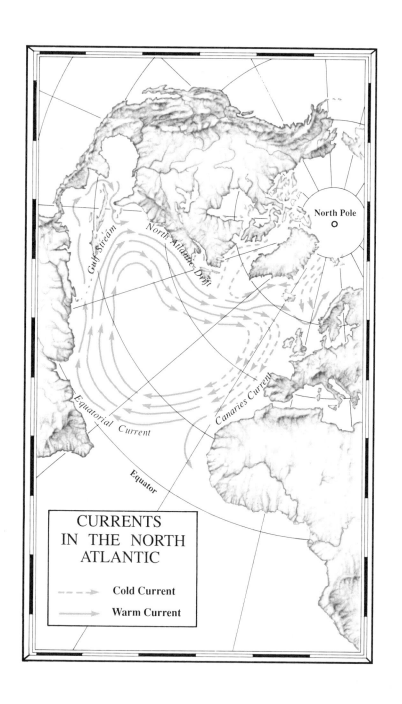

North Pole
O

Gulf Stream

North Atlantic Drift

Equatorial Current

Canaries Current

Equator

CURRENTS
IN THE NORTH
ATLANTIC

- - -> Cold Current

———> Warm Current

tering of waves, but actually the reed ship was so flexible that it bent with the movements of the waves.

Heyerdahl called his ship *Ra*, after the ancient Egyptian sun god. Ra is also the name given the sun by the inhabitants of Polynesia, islands in the South Pacific thousands of miles from Egypt.

When the ship was built, Heyerdahl signed on a crew of seven and set sail from the northwestern tip of Africa bound for Central America. Partway through the voyage, the ship started to fall apart. The journey was never completed. A design flaw was discovered, and a second ship, *Ra 2*, was built that incorporated some design changes.

Ra 2 picked up the Canary current from the west coast of Africa that flows across the Atlantic in a curve and sweeps into the Gulf of Mexico. With the wind plus the help of the current, the ship eventually reached the Gulf of Mexico. The Canary current is the same one that Christopher Columbus picked up on his voyages to the New World. *Ra 2* covered about 58 miles (93 km) a day—about as much as a simple sailboat would cover today—and took two months to complete its voyage.

This time the ship did not fall apart. "I have no theory but that a reed boat is seaworthy and that the Atlantic is a conveyer," Heyerdahl says in his book *The Ra Expeditions*. In other words, he had proved that if one found the right Atlantic current and had favorable sailing conditions, crossing the Atlantic in a reed ship was possible, and that the Egyptians could have made such a voyage.

*Taking leave of Queen Isabella
and King Ferdinand, Columbus
departs for his first voyage.*

8

COLUMBUS
AND THE AGE
OF DISCOVERY

Columbus wasn't the first European to visit the New World, but he was instrumental in demonstrating that there is more to our planet than what had been believed. He proved what had only been hinted at in early maps. His historic voyages were followed by other voyages, all of which were to form the Age of Discovery.

Columbus undertook his voyages for economic reasons. His trips were financed by the King and Queen of Spain for the purpose of finding an ocean trade route to India. The usual route taken to bring silks and spices from India to Europe was overland, by caravan from China and India to the eastern Mediterranean and from Italy to the rest of Europe. Taxes were imposed every step of the way. By the time the goods reached the market, even the rich could barely afford them.

If a Spaniard could find a direct sea route to India, then Spain would control the market. They could beat the current high prices and still turn a handsome profit on each piece of merchandise.

Columbus seemed certain that he would find India by sailing to the west. Some maps showed a large land mass to the west of Europe. Why did Columbus head for the southernmost part of this land mass? People knew that India must be a very hot country since spices do not grow surrounded by snow and ice. Columbus reasoned that India was a large continent and that the Vikings had discovered only its northernmost part. He believed that in the south he would find the goods he was looking for, goods that would make both himself and his king and queen wealthy.

He began his trip by picking up the Canary current. When he finally reached what he thought was southern India, he did indeed find a hot climate and spices. Until the day he died he thought he had reached India. That's why he called the natives of the Antilles Indians.

Columbus made three additional voyages to the New World, each time believing he was somewhere in the Far East. But despite his own mistaken ideas and although he had reached the wrong side of the world, his voyage played a major role in the subsequent colonization of a part of the world until then unknown to those who did not already live there. This colonization was to have an even greater effect on the New World than the original colonization by the people who came over the land bridge from Asia thousands upon thousands of years ago.

FOR FURTHER READING

Armstrong, Richard. *Early Mariners*. New York: Praeger, 1968.

Asche, Geoffrey, Thor Heyerdahl, Helge Ingstad, J. V. Luce, Betty J. Meggers, and Brigitta L. Wallace. *The Quest for America*. New York: Praeger, 1971.

Baity, Elizabeth C. *Americans Before Columbus*. New York: Crowell, 1967.

Benson, Elizabeth E. *The Maya World*. New York: Crowell, 1967.

Brent, Peter. *The Viking Saga*. New York: Putnam, 1965.

Chapman, Paul H. *The Norse Discovery of North America*. Atlanta, GA: One Candle Press, 1981.

Coe, Michael D. *America's First Civilization*. New York: American Heritage, 1968.

Davies, Nigel. *Voyagers to the New World*. New York: Morrow, 1979.

Enterline, James R. *Viking America*. Garden City, N.Y.: Doubleday, 1972.

Fagan, Brian M. *The Great Journey: The People of Ancient America*. New York: Thames and Hudson, 1987.

Folsom, Franklin. *America's Ancient Treasures*. New York: McNally, 1907.

Heyerdahl, Thor. *Early Man and the Ocean*. Garden City, N.Y.: Doubleday, 1978.

———. *The RA Expeditions*. Garden City, N.Y.: Doubleday, 1971.

Jennings, Jesse D., ed. *Ancient North Americans*. San Francisco: W. H. Freeman, 1983.

Jones, Gwyn. *The Vikings.* Rev. ed. New York: Oxford University Press, 1984.

Magnusson, M. *The Vinland Sagas.* New York: Oxford University Press, 1980.

Marrin, Albert. *Aztecs and Spaniards: Cortes and the Conquest of Mexico.* New York: Atheneum, 1986.

Meyer, Caroline, and Charles Gallencamp. *The Mystery of the Ancient Maya.* New York: Atheneum, 1985.

Morison, Samuel E. *The European Discovery of America.* New York: Oxford University Press, 1971.

Severin, Timothy. *The Brendan Voyage.* New York: McGraw-Hill, 1978.

Van Sertima, Ivan. *They Came Before Columbus.* New York: Random House, 1976.

INDEX